TRANSYLVANIA
TRAVEL GUIDE 2023

The Heart of Romania: Uncover the Rich History and Hidden Gems of Transylvania. An Insider's Guide to this Enchanting Wonderland

NICOLAS MENDEZ

All Right Reserved!

No Part of this book may be reproduced, stored in a retrieval system, or transmitted in any form or by any means, electronic or mechanical, photocopying, recording or otherwise, without the prior written permission of the copyright owner

Copyright © Nicolas Mendez, 2023

TRANSYLVANIA TRAVEL GUIDE 2023

Table of Contents

INTRODUCTION

GETTING STARTED: Your Transylvanian Journey Begins Here

GETTING TO TRANSYLVANIA: Your Journey to the Heart of Romania

EXPLORING TRANSYLVANIA: Unveiling the Mystique and Majesty

TRANSYLVANIA'S TOP ATTRACTIONS: Unveiling the Gems of the Land Beyond the Forest

OUTDOOR ADVENTURES IN TRANSYLVANIA: Embrace Nature's Playground

CULTURAL EXPERIENCES IN TRANSYLVANIA

ACCOMMODATION IN TRANSYLVANIA:

Where Comfort Meets Tradition

DINING AND CUISINE IN TRANSYLVANIA: A Culinary Journey Through Tradition and Flavour

PRACTICAL INFORMATION FOR TRAVELING IN TRANSYLVANIA: Navigating Your Journey with Ease

TRAVEL RESOURCES TO MAKE YOUR TRANSYLVANIAN ADVENTURE BETTER

APPENDIX: Essential Reference for Your Transylvanian Journey

CONCLUSION: Farewell to Transylvania, Until We Meet Again

BONUS: WHEN VISITING TRANSYLVANIA, AVOID THESE 15 THINGS AT ALL COSTS.

INTRODUCTION

Welcome to the "**Transylvania Travel Guide 2023**," your entryway to Romania's captivating interior. Your passport to one of Europe's most alluring and myth-filled areas is this well-prepared book. As you set off on your Transylvanian trip, you'll learn about a region rich in history where majestic scenery, quaint towns, and ancient castles are waiting.

The goal of our journey is to thoroughly immerse you in Transylvania's distinctive fusion of mythology and history, from the enigmatic legends surrounding Bran's Dracula's Castle to the exquisitely decorated monasteries of Bucovina.

This book contains everything you need, whether you're an adventurous traveler looking for outdoor experiences in the Carpathian Mountains or a cultural aficionado wanting to sample traditional

Romanian food and take part in lively local festivals.

Join us on a discovery voyage as we reveal the finest of Transylvania and provide helpful recommendations, insider knowledge, and cultural insights to help you have a great trip. Prepare to discover, engage in, and be amazed by Transylvania's enchantment in 2023.

Welcome to Transylvania

Transylvania, located in the center of Romania, is a region with enthralling natural beauty, a lengthy history, and folklore that has captivated the attention of tourists from all over the globe. This **"Transylvania Travel Guide 2023"** is your key to discovering this enchanted region's mysteries. Transylvania has a lot to offer, whether you're a history nerd, an adventure seeker, a foodie, or just a visitor looking for new experiences.

Regarding This Guide

To make your trip to Transylvania as enjoyable as possible, we pledge to provide you with a thorough and authentic resource. This book is the product of in-depth investigation, in-depth knowledge of the area, and a love for promoting the finest of this area. This book stands out due to its focus on both well-known tourist attractions and undiscovered treasures that genuinely distinguish Transylvania.

How to Use This Guide

A strange place might be intimidating to navigate, but do not worry! This manual's user-friendly and effective design will help you get the most out of your Transylvanian journey.

Transylvania is a complex area with several subregions, each of which offers a unique experience. The travel guide is divided into several locations, such as Brasov and Central Transylvania, Cluj-Napoca, Northwestern Transylvania, and more, to make it easier for you to tour effectively. You may obtain information that is relevant to you by simply selecting your destination.

Attractions and Activities: We've highlighted the top tourist destinations, outdoor activities, cultural experiences, and more within each area. You'll discover thorough information and suggestions on everything from trekking in beautiful landscapes to experiencing local customs to touring medieval castles.

Accommodations and Dining: We are aware that your choice of accommodations and meals will have a significant impact on how you enjoy your trip. Discover a variety of lodging choices, from inviting guest houses to opulent resorts. Discover Transylvania's gastronomic delights, from hearty traditional cuisine to elegant dining establishments.

Practical advice: Travel arrangements may be complicated, particularly in a foreign place. You may discover helpful advice on money and currency, language, safety, health, regional traditions, and connections in the practical information area.

Your travel will be made easier and a flawless experience is guaranteed by this area. Suggested applications and websites, a reading list, and a packing list are all included in our travel guide. These tools are intended to make your vacation more enjoyable and convenient.

Important Travel Advice

Although Transylvania is a fascinating place, it has its own unique set of concerns, just like any other travel journey. As you get ready for your trip to

Transylvania, keep these important travel advice in mind:

Best Time to Visit: Transylvania experiences seasonal climatic changes. While the beautiful summer months of June through August are best for outdoor activities, the winter months of December through February are good for those who like snow sports. There are fewer people and nicer temperatures in the spring and fall.

Visa and Entry Requirements: You could require a visa to enter Romania depending on your nationality. Make sure your passport is valid for at least six months after the date you want to go and research the necessary visas well in advance.

Having Adequate Insurance that covers unexpected occurrences like medical crises and trip cancellations is strongly advised. Throughout your travels, it offers you comfort.

Planning Your Trip's Budget: Transylvania has a variety of alternatives to fit various travel budgets. Consider the prices of lodging, dining, entertainment, and transportation as you plan your spending.

Getting there: You may fly into important airports like Cluj-Napoca, Brasov, or Sibiu depending on where you are. As an alternative, think about taking a scenic train or bus ride to take in the scenery.

Local transit: There are effective and affordable public transit systems. Renting a vehicle might provide you greater freedom if you want to visit rural locations.

Language and Interaction: English and other languages are widely spoken in Romania, even though Romanian is the official tongue. This is particularly true in tourist destinations. For a more immersive experience, it's beneficial to understand a few fundamental Romanian expressions.

Transylvania is typically a safe place to visit in terms of **safety and health**. However, use common sense and be alert to your surroundings as you would anyplace else. Make sure you are up to date on any essential immunizations and have any necessary prescriptions.

Local Customs & Etiquette: Respect the traditions and customs of the area to better understand it. A positive outlook and a desire to interact with locals can improve your experience.

Internet & Connectivity: Wi-Fi is readily accessible in hotels, restaurants, and cafés, so you can stay connected with ease. When traveling, think about getting a local SIM card for internet access.

You'll be ready to start your Transylvanian vacation by remembering this important travel advice. Transylvania provides a voyage full of life-changing experiences and discoveries, whether you're seeing ancient castles, trekking through beautiful landscapes, or indulging in delectable Romanian food. Welcome to a place where myths come to life and where there is always an adventure to be had.

GETTING STARTED: Your Transylvanian Journey Begins Here

An experience that offers beautiful scenery, a deep history, and folklore that has captivated people for generations is traveling to Transylvania, the heart of Romania. Making the most of your vacation requires careful preparation. The essential details you need to launch your Transylvanian excursion are provided in this part, "**Getting Started**," of the guide.

Organizing Your Travel

Setting the scene for your experience is the first step in organizing a vacation to Transylvania. Each step is essential to ensure a seamless and pleasurable experience, from choosing the best time to travel to comprehending visa requirements and planning your trip's budget.

When to visit

The varied climate of Transylvania provides a range of seasonal experiences. Your choices and areas of interest will determine when is the best time to visit:

I) **Summer (June to August):** When the weather is nice and pleasant, this is the busiest travel period. It is ideal for outdoor pursuits like hiking and discovering the area's breathtaking sights. Popular destinations are likely to get more visitors around this period.

II) The shoulder seasons of **spring (March to May) and fall (September to November)** provide warmer temperatures, fewer tourists, and a more laid-back ambiance. Without the summer crowds, it's a great time to go sightseeing and take in the local culture.

III) Snowy (December to February):
Transylvania, particularly the hilly parts, turns into a snowy wonderland. For fans of winter activities like skiing and snowboarding, this is the time of year. The Christmas season enhances the area's festive attractiveness.

When deciding when is the perfect time for your Transylvanian vacation, take into account your hobbies and the experiences you want.

Entry Requirements and Visas

Understanding Romania's visa and entrance regulations is essential before packing your bags and traveling to Transylvania. Depending on your country, these criteria may change. To remember, have the following in mind:

I) **EU and EEA Citizens**: With a current passport or national ID card, you may enter Romania if you are a citizen of the European Union (EU) or the European Economic Area (EEA). For brief visits, visas are not necessary.

II) **Citizens of nations outside the EU/EEA**: Tourists from these nations may require a visa to visit Romania. Your country of citizenship will determine the kind of visa and the application procedure. It's essential to confirm the prerequisites well in advance and, if required, apply for the proper visa.

III) **Validity of Passport**: Ensure that your passport is valid for at least six months after the day you want to leave Romania.

IV) It is advised to check the **official website of the Romanian Ministry of Foreign Affairs** or contact the Romanian embassy or consulate in your area to remain current on visa requirements and entrance criteria.

Travel Insurance

Your safety net while visiting unfamiliar places is travel insurance. In the event of unforeseen circumstances, it offers comfort of mind and financial security. For your trip to Transylvania, travel insurance is necessary because of the following:

I) **Medical Coverage**: In case of sickness or accident while traveling, travel insurance normally pays for medical costs. It makes sure you get the proper medical attention without having to pay a lot of money.

II) **Trip Cancellation/Interruption**: Because of the irrationality of life, anything might go wrong. If you must cancel or shorten your trip due to unforeseeable circumstances, travel insurance may pay you for non-refundable trip charges.

III) Travel insurance may help you replace necessary things and pay for your stuff if your baggage is lost, damaged, or stolen.

IV) **Emergency aid**: Having access to round-the-clock emergency aid while you're gone from home may save your life. Frequently, services like medical evacuation and help with misplaced papers are covered by travel insurance.

Read the policy completely before buying it to see what it covers and any exclusions. Make sure it satisfies your unique requirements and the activities you have planned for your Transylvanian excursion.

Budgeting your Trip

Planning a trip's budget is an essential component, and Transylvania has a variety of alternatives to fit various budgets. When making travel plans on a budget, keep the following things in mind:

Accommodations: Transylvania has a wide range of lodging alternatives, from opulent resorts and boutique hotels to hostels and guesthouses that are affordable. Your decision will have a big effect on your total spending plan.

Food & Dining: There are many options to enjoy both traditional Romanian food and delicacies from other countries in Transylvania. Local eateries, fancy dining establishments, or street cuisine may all be chosen as your eating options.

Plan your activities and must-see places before you go sightseeing. Check to see if you qualify for one of the many attractions that offer student and senior discounts on admission.

Consider your alternatives for **getting around**, including planes, trains, and local transportation inside Transylvania. In general, public transit is economical and effective.

Miscellaneous charges: Take into account spending for entertainment, mementos, and unanticipated charges.

Finding the right balance between seeing the finest of Transylvania and living within your means is crucial. To make sure your funds match your vacation objectives, do some research and make a plan in advance.

Keep in mind that careful preparation creates the foundation for an unforgettable trip as you start on your Transylvanian excursion. You may maximize your stay in this interesting location by being aware of the best times to go, the visa requirements, getting travel insurance and setting a sensible spending limit. Transylvania provides a trip that is full of discovery and amazement, whether you want to hike through beautiful landscapes, see historic castles, or indulge in regional cuisine.

GETTING TO TRANSYLVANIA:
Your Journey to the Heart of Romania

The first thrilling stage of your journey to experience this magical area is getting to Transylvania. Each means of transportation provides different experiences, whether you're traveling to or from Transylvania by plane, rail, bus, or contemplating a rental car. Additionally, after you've arrived, local transportation choices including public transit, car rentals, cycling, and walking may assist you in navigating and allowing you to fully experience the beauty and culture of Transylvania.

Travel by Air

The most practical method of entry into Transylvania for many visitors from outside is via flying. Numerous airports serve Transylvania, with Cluj International Airport (CLU) and Sibiu

International Airport (SBZ) serving as two of the main entry points.

One of the busiest airports in the area is **Cluj International Airport (CLU),** which is close to Cluj-Napoca in Northwestern Transylvania. As a result of its links to significant European cities, it is a well-liked starting location for tourists touring this region of Transylvania.

Located close to Sibiu in Southern Transylvania, **Sibiu International Airport (SBZ)** offers access to the region's southern districts. Cities like Vienna, Munich, and Bucharest are easily accessible from there.

You may use taxis, airport shuttles, rental cars, and other modes of transportation from these airports to get to your destination in Transylvania. These airports are home to the majority of major automobile rental firms, providing you the freedom to explore the area at your speed.

Bus and Train Options

A unique experience awaits you if you prefer a picturesque and leisurely journey: taking the train or bus to Transylvania. Transylvania is connected to other major cities and areas via Romania's large rail network. Here are some crucial things to remember:

a) **Trains**: A vast railway network is run by Romanian Railways (**CFR Călători**). From other regions of Romania and nearby nations like Hungary and Bulgaria, trains offer a convenient and environmentally responsible method to get to cities like Cluj-Napoca, Brasov, and Sibiu. For nighttime travel, sleeper trains are an option that provides comfort and accommodations.

b) **Buses**: Long-distance buses are another affordable option for getting to Transylvania. Routes to significant regional cities are provided by organizations like FlixBus and Eurolines. You may take in the scenery while traveling by bus, which is a cost-effective choice.

c) **Local Trains and Buses:** Local trains and buses link smaller towns and villages across Transylvania. These may be a great opportunity to discover off-the-beaten-track locations and encounter real rural life.

Driving in Transylvania

Consider driving in Transylvania if you want freedom and independence on your trip. The area is the perfect place for a road trip because of its well-kept road system and beautiful scenery. The following are some crucial considerations:

I) Make sure you have a **valid driver's license** that is accepted in Romania. If your license is not in English or Romanian, an International Driving Permit (IDP) may be necessary.

II) **Traffic Regulations**: Be aware that Romanian traffic regulations may not be the same as those in your native country. Use seat belts at all times, drive on the correct side of the road, and obey speed restrictions.

III) **Road Conditions**: Transylvania's main thoroughfares are generally in decent shape, however, some rural regions may have smaller roads and sporadic potholes. Drive carefully, particularly while in a hilly area.

IV) **Fuel & Gas Stations**: Transylvania has easy access to both gasoline and diesel fuel. Self-service petrol stations are widespread, although some can only take cash, so have some on hand.

V) **Parking spaces** are available in the majority of towns and cities, some of which are charged. Search for appropriate parking areas and abide by local laws.

VI) **GPS and Maps**: Transylvania is well-suited for using GPS navigation systems, although it's a good idea to carry paper maps or a backup system in case of connection problems.

Take your time and see Transylvania at your leisure, keeping in mind that the region's picturesque scenery and historical attractions make for delightful journeys.

Local Transportation

You'll want effective local transportation choices to visit the region's attractions, cities, and scenic countryside after arriving in Transylvania, whether by flight, rail, bus, or automobile.

Using Public Transit

The cities and villages of Transylvania may be reached efficiently and affordably via public transit. The main forms of public transportation are as follows:

Bus and tram networks are well-developed in the majority of Transylvania's cities. They provide easy access to popular destinations, neighborhoods, and business regions.

In metropolitan areas, **taxis** are readily accessible. Make sure the taxi has a functional meter, or decide on a fee before the trip. In certain places, using a ride-hailing app like Uber may also be an alternative.

Metro: The metro system in Bucharest, the country's capital, offers effective local transit.

Access to high places and hiking routes is made possible in hilly areas like Brasov and Sinaia by funicular and cable cars.

Renting a Car

If you choose to hire a vehicle locally rather than at the airport, rental businesses are accessible in Transylvania's major towns and cities. You may go to off-the-beaten-path destinations, explore off-the-beaten-path sites, and take beautiful drives by renting a vehicle. Remember the following:

Driving License: Before hiring a vehicle, make sure you have all necessary documentation, including your driver's license and passport.

Consider renting insurance to protect against accidents or damages that may occur while you are renting a vehicle.

Traffic Regulations: When driving in Transylvania, abide by all local traffic laws. Be mindful of any parking restrictions and speed limits.

Gas stations are easily accessible, and gasoline costs are fair. Pay close attention to the different fuel kinds (gasoline, diesel), and choose the right one for your rental vehicle.

Walking and Cycling

The finest ways to see Transylvania's picturesque scenery and quaint towns are by bicycle or on foot. Here are some tips for maximizing these environmentally beneficial forms of transportation:

Cycling: Both on- and off-road cycling trails are available in several Transylvanian locations. Bringing your bike or renting one locally are also options. The Transfagarasan Highway may be explored on a bicycle for a spectacular experience.

Walking is a lovely way to discover medieval districts, cobblestone lanes, and bustling marketplaces in cities like Sibiu, Brasov, and Sighișoara. The Carpathian Mountains include hiking paths that provide breathtaking scenery and clean mountain air for outdoor lovers.

Make sure you have the proper equipment, maps, knowledge of the area, and information on the weather before starting a bike or hiking trip. The greatest way to see Transylvania's natural beauty and rich history is to go slowly on foot or by bicycle.

To sum up, Transylvania provides a variety of transportation choices to accommodate different tastes and travel habits. Transylvania offers

something to offer any tourist, whether they like the ease of flying,
the beautiful route of trains and buses, the independence of driving, or the eco-friendly discovery of cycling and walking. once you get there

EXPLORING TRANSYLVANIA: Unveiling the Mystique and Majesty

Travelers are drawn to Transylvania by its captivating fusion of history, tradition, and natural beauty, which lies tucked away in the center of Romania. There is a wealth of experiences to be had in this varied area, including historic castles, quaint towns, and breathtaking vistas. We'll go around Transylvania in this part by looking at its numerous areas, each of which has its attractions.

Transylvanian regions

The wide and varied area of Transylvania is renowned for its beautiful scenery and cultural diversity. It is sometimes separated into several smaller sections, each of which has its beauty. Let's explore the main areas of Transylvania:

Northwestern Transylvania and Cluj-Napoca

Cluj-Napoca is a dynamic city with a rich history and a young vitality. It serves as the unofficial capital of Northwestern Transylvania. St. Michael's Church and the Banffy Palace are only two examples of outstanding architecture that showcases a bygone age. The city's vibrant cultural sector, busy markets, and plenty of cafés and restaurants all contribute to the dynamic environment.

Turda: Located not far from Cluj-Napoca, Turda is known for its magnificent salt mine, which has been converted into a one-of-a-kind underground entertainment park. Enter the Earth's interior to discover this bizarre underground environment.

The Apuseni Mountains, a sanctuary for outdoor enthusiasts, are located in Northwestern Transylvania. There are several hiking and caving options, with attractions like the Turda Gorges and the Scarisoara Ice Cave as highlights.

Central Transylvania and Brasov

Brasov is a charming city with a long history and a well-preserved medieval town, nestled at the foot of the Carpathian Mountains. A must-see feature are the **recognizable Black Church**, **Council Square**, and the **majestic Bran Castle** (sometimes connected to Dracula).

Poiana Brasov: Just outside of Brasov, Poiana Brasov is known for its world-class skiing in the winter and for being a verdant mountain getaway in the summer. It provides leisure, skiing, and hiking in stunning natural settings.

The Transfagarasan Highway: Often cited as one of the world's most picturesque drives, this road runs through the Carpathian Mountains and provides access to hiking trails, beautiful lakes, and spectacular landscapes.

Sibiu and Southern Transylvania

Sibiu: One of Southern Transylvania's highlights is the charming and historically rich city of Sibiu. A UNESCO World Heritage Site, it is a well-preserved medieval center. Wander through the Brukenthal National Museum, see the panoramic views from the renowned Council Tower, and wander around the ancient city walls.

Sighișoara: This historical treasure is well-known for its intact fortress, which is included as a UNESCO World Heritage Site. In addition, Vlad the Impaler, the historical person who served as the model for Bram Stoker's Dracula, was born in Sighisoara.

Alba Iulia: The magnificent Alba Carolina Citadel, a masterpiece of Vauban military construction, is located in the city of Alba Iulia. You may see its well-preserved bastions and churches and experience history in action there.

Region of the Maramures

Maramures: The Maramures area, which is a portion of Transylvania's north, is a location where customs and folklore are alive and well. You may visit the charming wooden churches with high spires, the vibrant festivals, and the well-known Merry Cemetery, where the gravestones are inscribed with witty and sometimes colorful epitaphs.

Steam Mocanita: Take a trip through time on board the Mocanita, a narrow-gauge steam train that travels through the breathtaking Vaser Valley and provides a look into rural life and untainted scenery.

The Bucovina Region

Bucovina: Located in northeastern Transylvania, this area is known for its breathtaking painted monasteries. The vivid paintings at these UNESCO World Heritage Sites, such as those in Voronet, Moldovita, and Sucevita, tell biblical and historical tales.

The area of Bucovina is entered via the city of **Suceava**. Explore the stunning Suceava Fortress, which was important to medieval history.

Lacul Rosu (Red Lake) is a tranquil alpine lake with an intriguing past that is tucked away in the Carpathian Mountains. Its name comes from a historic natural disaster that happened when a landslide imprisoned tree trunks in the lake, giving it a distinctive scarlet tint.

Peeling back the layers of history and tradition one place at a time is what exploring Transylvania is like. Transylvania offers a distinctive experience waiting for you around every corner, whether you're drawn to the medieval allure of towns like Sibiu and Brasov, fascinated by the dynamic traditions of Maramures, or moved by the tranquil beauty of the painted monasteries of Bucovina.

Enjoy the regional food, interact with the welcoming inhabitants, and immerse yourself in the stories and traditions that have defined Transylvania's character as you travel across these areas. The Transylvanian tapestry is enhanced by each location, giving your tour an exciting exploration of this legendary country.

TRANSYLVANIA'S TOP ATTRACTIONS: Unveiling the Gems of the Land Beyond the Forest

The historical and mythical area of Transylvania is home to a variety of alluring attractions. Transylvania attracts visitors with its diverse array of activities, which range from breathtaking drives through the Carpathian Mountains to historic castles and strongholds. We'll look at a few of the main attractions that help Transylvania stand out as a travel destination in this section.

(Dracula's Castle) Bran Castle
Location: Bran

Bran Castle, often known as **"Dracula's Castle,"** is one of Transylvania's most recognizable and lasting emblems. This old castle, which is tucked away in the gorgeous Carpathian Mountains, radiates an air of mystery and intrigue. The castle has become a must-see destination despite not being Vlad the Impaler's original home, the historical character who served as the model for Bram Stoker's Dracula.

You'll be taken back in time to a realm of medieval beauty as you wander around the castle's hallways and chambers. The towers, hidden corridors, and decorated apartments of the castle provide an insight into its extensive past. Avoid missing the beautiful panoramic views of the surrounding area that may be seen from the castle's turrets.

The Bran Castle Museum is located there, thus its attractiveness goes beyond its association with Dracula. Here, you may learn about Vlad the Impaler, see exhibits that highlight the area's culture, and dig into the history of Transylvania.

Peleş Castle
Location: Sinaia

A monument to Romania's regal past, **Peleș Castle** is a great work of European architecture. This magnificent Neo-Renaissance castle is a sight to see and can be found in the lovely town of Sinaia, at the base of the Bucegi Mountains.

Peleș Castle, commissioned by Romania's King Carol I in the late 19th century, is a fusion of architectural styles with fine carvings, stained glass windows, and opulent interiors. You'll be mesmerized as soon as you enter by the lavishness and meticulous attention to detail that each area exudes. The Grand Armory, the Music Room, and the majestic Concert Hall are highlights.

The park that encircles the castle, which has terraces, sculptures, and strolling trails, adds to its allure. A voyage into the realm of aristocracy, fine art, and magnificent architecture awaits visitors at Peleș Castle.

Transfagarasan Highway
Location: Mountains of the Fagaras

There is no other highway like the Transfagarasan Highway. This serpentine mountain road, which weaves its way through the majestic Fagaras Mountains and reaches heights that give breathtaking panoramas, is often referred to as one of the world's most picturesque drives.

The highway, which was originally designed as a tactical military route, today attracts tourists looking for beautiful scenery and adventure. You'll pass through tunnels, bridges, and hairpin twists that lead to stunning alpine lakes and hiking paths as you go.
 At 2,034 meters above sea level, Balea Lake provides an opportunity to soak in the breathtaking surroundings and possibly even have a hearty lunch at the neighboring lodge.

For hikers, photographers, and wildlife lovers, the **Transfagarasan Highway** is a paradise. This picturesque road guarantees an amazing adventure into the heart of the Carpathian Mountains whether you explore it by vehicle, motorbike, or on foot.

Citadel of Sighișoara
Location: Sighișoara

The center of Transylvania is home to the picturesque and amazingly well-preserved medieval town of Sighisoara Citadel. It is often described as one of Europe's best-preserved inhabited citadels and is a UNESCO World Heritage Site.

The recognizable Clock Tower, which watches over the town's historic core, serves as Sighisoara's focal point. You will come across vibrant homes, guarded walls, and magical squares as you stroll over cobblestone streets. Don't miss the museum-turned-birthplace of Vlad the Impaler, the historical man who served as the basis for the Dracula story.

The Clock Tower may be climbed for sweeping views of Sighisoara and the surrounding area. There are galleries, artisan workshops, and cultural events in the town, which also has a thriving arts scene.

When you visit Sighisoara Citadel, it's like traveling back in time to the Middle Ages. Here, history, architecture, and mythology come together to create an enthralling environment.

Bucovina's Painted Monasteries
Location: Bucovina region.

The spectacular ecclesiastical structures known as The Painted Monasteries of Bucovina are covered in elaborate murals that represent biblical themes, saints, and historical events. The scenic Bucovina area of northern Romania is home to these UNESCO World Heritage Sites.

Each monastery's façade is covered in vivid paintings, making each one a work of beauty and a haven for the soul. The most well-known painted monasteries are Sucevita, Moldovita, and Voronet. The distinctive hue of intense blue known as **"Voronet blue"** has maintained its brightness for generations.

Aside from being a spiritual experience, visiting these monasteries offers the chance to see the creative ability of the medieval artists who produced these works of art. The Painted Monasteries of Bucovina are a one-of-a-kind and touching attraction because they combine religious devotion and artistic expression.

The Merry Cemetery
Location: Sapanta

There are no other cemeteries like the Merry Cemetery in the Sapanta village. Death is honored in this setting with comedy, vibrant colors, and elaborate wooden crosses that detail the lives of people laid to rest there.

The Merry Cemetery, created by local artist Stan Ioan Patras, is a representation of the distinctive culture and customs of the area. A vibrant cross with a humorous inscription and a painted scene that exemplifies the life, career, or personality of the departed marks each grave. The witty and moving lines provide a window into Maramures residents' daily lives.

An insightful and touching experience is visiting the Merry Cemetery. It serves as both a celebration of life and a reminder that happiness, humor, and a feeling of community are possible even in death.

Finally, Transylvania's finest tourist destinations provide an enthralling fusion of the region's history, culture, and natural beauty. Transylvania invites you to set out on a journey of exploration, inspiration, and wonder, whether you choose to visit the legendary halls of Bran Castle, take in the splendor of Peleș Castle, go on a scenic road trip along the Transfagarasan Highway, meander through the medieval streets of Sighisoara Citadel, take in the vivid frescoes of Bucovina's painted monasteries, or reflect on life and death at the Merry Cemetery.

Each of These sites are evidence of the area's rich past and its lasting power to enthrall visitors from all over the globe.

OUTDOOR ADVENTURES IN TRANSYLVANIA: Embrace Nature's Playground

Outdoor enthusiasts may play in Transylvania's stunning landscapes and untouched wilderness. Transylvania's stunning natural surroundings entice visitors to discover its delights, from harrowing animal encounters to arduous mountain routes.

We'll delve into the world of outdoor adventures in this part, including activities like hiking and trekking, animal observation, skiing and other winter sports, caving, and spelunking.

Trekking & Hiking

With a vast network of paths crisscrossing its varied topography, Transylvania is a hiker's dream. Whether you're a seasoned hiker or just a casual walker, Transylvania has a hiking trail to suit your interests and degree of fitness.

Carpathian Mountains: The Carpathians provide many trekking options with their undulating landscapes and high summits. While the Apuseni Mountains provide softer trails through woods, valleys, and caves, the Fagaras Mountains, which are the site of the Transfagarasan Highway, offer strenuous high-altitude excursions.

Piatra Craiului National Park is a refuge for hikers and is renowned for its stunning limestone hills. Adventurers who complete the strenuous Zarnesti Gorges path are rewarded with breathtaking views of the mountains and surrounding areas.

Retezat National Park is a wilderness made up of craggy peaks, glacial lakes, and alpine meadows. A network of paths is available for hikers to explore, including the well-known circuit around Bucura Lake.

Bucegi Mountains: With famous locations like the Babele and the Sphinx, and rock formations with interesting tales, the Bucegi Mountains offer a variety of moderate and difficult excursions.

Maramures: Hiking through picture-perfect towns and verdant woods is available in the northern part of the Romanian country, and it's much more charming to come across local customs.

Be equipped with the right tools, maps, and a spirit of adventure before you go out into Transylvania's woods. Transylvania's paths will take you to amazing experiences whether you hike for the panoramic vistas, the adventure of discovery, or a closer relationship with nature

Wildlife Watching

The woods, marshes, and mountains of Transylvania provide crucial habitats for a wide variety of animals. There are several chances for tracking bears, birding, and other intriguing animal observations for wildlife aficionados.

Brown Bears: A sizable population of brown bears resides in Transylvania. You may see these magnificent animals in their native environment by taking a wildlife trip in places like the Carpathian Mountains or the Harghita region.

Birdwatching: A top location for birdwatching is the Danube Delta, a UNESCO World Heritage Site on the Transylvanian border. This wetland paradise is home to hundreds of bird species, including pelicans, herons, and swans.

Bison Reserve: A successful reintroduction of European bison has taken place in the Taurus Mountains in southern Transylvania. A rare opportunity to see these remarkable creatures is provided by a trip to the Tarcu Bison Reserve.

Join a wolf-tracking adventure in the Carpathians for a unique and engaging experience. You may follow knowledgeable guides to locations where you could see wolf tracks, droppings, or perhaps a fleeting sight of these elusive carnivores.

Wildlife Refuges: Transylvania is home to several protected areas and wildlife refuges where you may see a variety of birds, animals, and amphibians. Additionally, several of these locations provide educational programs and escorted excursions.

Maintain a respectful distance from all wildlife and observe it ethically. You may get up close and personal with the animals while avoiding upsetting them by using binoculars and telephoto lenses. The health of the animals and their natural environment should always come first.

Winter sports and skiing
Skiers and other fans of winter sports will find Transylvania to be the perfect location as it changes into a winter paradise. The area offers several different ski resorts as well as chances for snowboarding, snowshoeing, and other winter sports.

Poiana Brasov: One of the most well-liked ski areas in Transylvania is Poiana Brasov, which is close to the city of Brasov. It has well-maintained slopes, contemporary amenities, and a buzzing après-ski culture.

Peleș Castle is located near Sinaia, which is also a center for winter sports. Several slopes at the Sinaia Ski Resort are appropriate for skiers of all abilities.

The Maramures region's Borsa, with its immaculate slopes and breathtaking mountain environment, provides a distinctive skiing experience.

Muntele Mic: Muntele Mic, also known as Stara Planina, is a ski resort in the Carpathian Mountains that also offers snowboarding and snowshoeing options.

Balea Lake: During the winter, visitors may enjoy ice fishing and snow-related sports in a stunning alpine environment at Balea Lake, which is accessible by the Transfagarasan Highway.

The ski resorts in Transylvania provide a combination of winter activities and alpine splendor, whether you're an experienced skier or a novice snowboarder. For guests of all ability levels, a lot of resorts provide equipment rentals and training.

CULTURAL EXPERIENCES IN TRANSYLVANIA

Transylvania offers visitors a wealth of cultural events that encourage them to fully immerse themselves in the area's history in addition to its mesmerizing natural surroundings. Transylvania provides a richly varied cultural experience that is both unique and enlightening, including sampling traditional Romanian food, taking part in energetic festivals, visiting nearby markets, and learning about folklore and customs.

Romanian traditional cuisine

The various history and geographical influences of Romania are reflected in its food, and Transylvania is no exception. Take a gastronomic journey as you enjoy delicacies that have been honed over many years.

Mămăligă: This national cuisine of Romania is often contrasted with polenta. Mămăligă, a common dish made of cornmeal, is eaten as a side dish with a variety of ingredients, such as sour cream and cheese.

Sarmale: The standard filling for these mouthwatering cabbage rolls is a combination of rice, spices, ground meat, and pig. After that, they are cooked slowly and often served with sour cream.

Mici: These tiny, grilled sausages, sometimes called "**mititei**," are seasoned with garlic, paprika, and other spices. They are a barbeque staple that is often eaten with mustard.

Ciorbă: Ciorbă, or sour soups from Romania, is a cherished culinary heritage. Ciorbă de burtă (tripe soup) and ciorbă de perișoare (meatball soup) are two varieties.

Mămăligă with brânză și smântână: Mămăligă is a delicious dish where the cornmeal is served as a porridge-like foundation, topped with cheese and a hefty dollop of smântână.

Desserts: With treats like papayas (fried doughnuts stuffed with jam and sour cream), cozonac (sweet bread), and plăcinte (pastries stuffed with sweet or savory ingredients), Transylvania is a sweet tooth's heaven.

Local wines are available in Transylvania, particularly the Fetească Neagră and Grasă de Cotnari kinds, which go well with Romanian cuisine.

Consider going to a traditional restaurant or looking for neighborhood eateries and street food sellers to properly appreciate Transylvanian cuisine. A glimpse of the cultural uniqueness of the area will be offered through the substantial cuisine and rich spices.

Events and Festivals

The cultural calendar of Transylvania is characterized by a vibrant tapestry of festivals and events that honor customs, the arts, and local traditions. Attending these events offers a fascinating glimpse into the vibrant cultural life of the area.

One of the most renowned film festivals in Romania is the **Transilvania International Film Festival (TIFF)**, which takes place in Cluj-Napoca. It features a broad variety of foreign and Romanian films and draws performers, directors, and movie lovers from all over the globe.

The streets and squares of Sibiu are turned into outdoor stages for the **acclaimed Sibiu**

International Theatre Festival (FITS). Classical theater as well as modern and experimental pieces are performed.

Imagine going to a music event in an underground salt mine, such as the **Turda Salt Mine Music event**. In the unearthly backdrop of the Turda Salt Mine, a variety of musical groups will perform at this one-of-a-kind event.

Folk Festivals: Transylvania is home to several festivals honoring folk art, music, and dance. These occasions often take place in quaint towns and include folklore and traditions from the area.

Horse-Drawn Cart Procession (Targu Mures): To honor the area's agricultural past, Targu Mures inhabitants adorn horse-drawn carts for this yearly procession in a variety of vibrant designs.

Medieval Festivals: Several Transylvanian villages and citadels host medieval celebrations that take tourists back in time. Reenactments, jousting contests, and artisan exhibitions may all be seen.

When organizing your trip to Transylvania, be sure to look at the festival schedules since these occasions provide a chance to interact with the locals and experience the artistic and creative expression of the area.

Local Markets

A genuine way to experience everyday life in Transylvania, enjoy fresh vegetables, and find handcrafted goods is to explore local markets.

The central market in Brasov, which features a colorful selection of local goods such as cheeses, fruits, and vegetables, is called Brașov Central

Market. It's the perfect location to sample regional cuisine and browse souvenir shops.

The market in Cluj-Napoca is a hive of activity where you can get everything from apparel and antiques to fresh fruit. Taste the local cheeses and cured meats while you can.

Sibiu Christmas Market: Sibiu Christmas Market is a spectacular experience if you're traveling during the holiday season. Enjoy classic foods such as gingerbread cookies, roasted chestnuts, and mulled wine.

Maramures Village marketplaces: In the Maramures' rural communities, you may find real marketplaces where residents exchange vegetables and handcrafted items. These marketplaces provide visitors with a look at everyday life in traditional Transylvania.

The Huet Square in Sibiu hosts the Sibiu Farmers' Market, which displays the agricultural abundance of the area, including fresh fruits, vegetables, and dairy products. It's a great area to mingle with the locals.

Craft markets may be found all around Transylvania, where local craftsmen sell their handcrafted ceramics, woodwork, textiles, and jewelry. These marketplaces are ideal for finding one-of-a-kind gifts.

You may interact with friendly people, sample seasonal cuisine, and learn about the workmanship that has been handed down through the decades by strolling around local markets.

Folklore and Traditions

The rich folklore and customs of Transylvania are closely entwined with its sense of cultural identity.

Immersion in these traditions may help you understand the history of the area and the resilient nature of its inhabitants.

Folk music and dance are essential components of Transylvanian culture. At festivals and gatherings, traditional dances like the hora and the călușari dance are often performed.

Storytelling: Myths, stories, and fairy tales abound in Transylvanian folklore. Listen to the natives tell tales about dragons, vampires, and other fantastical creatures.

Craftsmanship: In Transylvania, craftsmanship is highly valued. Visit workshops and talk to craftsmen who use generations-old methods to produce stunning wood carvings, fabrics, and ceramics.

Religious Traditions: The Eastern Orthodox Church and various forms of religion are central to many Transylvanian customs. A greater insight into the spirituality of the area may be gained by attending religious festivals and rituals.

Clothes: Special events and folk festivals still call for the wearing of traditional Transylvanian clothes, which are distinguished by elaborate needlework and vivid colors.

Rural Life: Visiting rural Transylvanian villages gives you the chance to see how people have lived there for decades. You may see customs including haymaking, sheepherding, and traditional culinary techniques.

Participating in these rituals, whether it be seeing a dance performance, hearing folklore, or making pottery, provides a window into the continuing traditions that characterize Transylvania's cultural history.

In conclusion, Transylvania is a region rich in cultural variety, where customs, food, festivals, and folklore all come together to weave a tapestry of impressions.

Transylvania invites you to embrace its cultural heritage and set out on a journey of discovery and connection with the area and its kind people, whether you choose to indulge in the flavors of traditional Romanian cuisine, immerse yourself in the lively festivities, wander local markets, or delve into centuries-old customs.

ACCOMMODATION IN TRANSYLVANIA: Where Comfort Meets Tradition

Finding the ideal lodging in Transylvania is about more than simply finding a place to sleep; it's also a chance to experience the welcoming culture of the area. From charming inns to historic hotels and even adventurous camping, Transylvania provides a wide variety of accommodation choices.

We'll look at the many sorts of lodging that are available, where to stay by area, inexpensive alternatives, opulent getaways, and some very unusual spots to call home during your Transylvanian vacation in this thorough guide.

Types of Accommodation

All sorts of guests may find accommodations in Transylvania that will fit their likes and budgets.

The following are some of the most typical hotel options in the area:

a) **Resorts and Hotels**

Overview: Transylvania offers a variety of lodging options, from small boutique hotels to expensive luxury resorts. They often provide a broad variety of facilities and services, such as dining establishments, spas, and tour guides.

Pros: For visitors searching for a stress-free stay, hotels and resorts are popular options because of comfort, convenience, and a variety of amenities.

Cons: More expensive rates in comparison to alternative lodging choices.

b) **Bed & Breakfasts (B&Bs)** and guesthouses

In general, guesthouses and B&Bs are owned by families and provide a more individualized and private experience. They often provide home-cooked meals with attractive décor.

Positives: The ability to interact with people and have genuine local experiences.

Cons: Fewer amenities than hotels; regional availability may be different.

c) **Hostels**

Overview: Hostels are inexpensive lodging options that often appeal to youthful tourists or those looking for a social setting. Both individual rooms and dormitory-style accommodations are available.

Pros: Affordable option, great for budget-conscious or lone travelers, and chances to meet other travelers.

Cons: Less privacy compared to alternative lodgings; not all age groups may find it appropriate.

d) **Glamping and camping**

Overview: Glamping (glamorous camping) and camping enable you to fully experience Transylvania's natural splendor. Bring your camping supplies or choose glamping tents furnished with luxurious facilities.

Advantages: A feeling of adventure, affordability, and being close to nature.

Cons: Remote camping sites with few amenities; glamping might cost more than typical camping.

Places to Stay

Accommodation by Region

Transylvania is a varied area with a variety of natural and cultural landmarks. Your interests and the kind of experiences you're looking for will play a big role in where you stay. Following are some important areas and their highlights:

Brasov and Area: The city of Brasov serves as a base for traveling to the Carpathian Mountains' ski areas. Stay here for quick access to Sibiu's lovely center, Bran Castle, and the Transfagarasan Highway.

In addition to providing a bustling metropolitan experience, **Cluj-Napoca** also provides a starting point for trips to the Turda Salt Mine and the Apuseni Mountains in Northwestern Transylvania.

Sibiu and Southern Transylvania: The old center of Sibiu, which has been kept effectively, is a UNESCO World Heritage Site. It's a great starting point for seeing southern Transylvania, including the historic Sighisoara and the breathtaking Fagaras Mountains.

Maramures: Staying at a traditional guesthouse in Maramures will provide a real rural experience. The wooden churches, wooden gates, and rich folklore of this area are well known.

Bucovina: The spectacular painted monasteries and attractive scenery of northern Romania are accessible from lodging in the Bucovina area.

Budget-Friendly options

There are many inexpensive lodging options available all around Transylvania for those on a tight budget. Think about these choices:

Hostels: The hostel sector in Transylvania is expanding, with inexpensive choices available in important towns like Cluj-Napoca, Brasov, and Sibiu.

Traditional inns: Particularly in rural locations, inns can have affordable prices. You'll have the opportunity to benefit from genuine Romanian hospitality.

Camping: One of the least expensive ways to stay in Transylvania is to camp. Several campsites provide inexpensive, basic amenities.

Utilize Internet booking tools to locate savings and exclusive deals at hotels and guesthouses.

Luxury Retreats

Transylvania has several sumptuous retreats where visitors looking for lavish experiences may luxuriate in comfort and first-rate service:

Historic Hotels: Reside in opulent historical hotels like the Hotel Ciprian in Sibiu or the Kronwell Hotel in Brasov, where the opulence of the present combines with the charm of the past.

Resorts: Expensive resorts with amenities including spa services, golf courses, and breathtaking mountain vistas including the Poiana Brasov Resort.

Countryside Retreats: Some rural locations are home to upscale villas and boutique hotels that provide peace, seclusion, and individualized services.

Staying in a castle will allow you to realize your aspirations of living in a fairytale. **The Count Kalnoky's Guesthouses** in Miclosoara is one of several Transylvanian castles that have been transformed into posh lodging.

Unique Stays

In addition, Transylvania provides a variety of unusual and out-of-the-ordinary lodgings for travelers seeking exceptional experiences:

Treehouse Retreats: In the remote Carpathian Mountains, take advantage of a stay in a treetop retreat.

Fortified churches in Transylvania: A few of these churches have converted their towers into guestrooms, providing a storied and evocative stay.

Homestays in traditional communities, such as those in the Maramures area, allow visitors to get a taste of rural life.

Staying in a cave hotel close to Turda will allow you to take part in a unique subterranean journey.

Eco-Friendly Lodges: Tourists who care about the environment may choose from a variety of eco-friendly lodgings that support sustainability and conservation.

You may customize your trip to Transylvania to fit your interests and financial limitations by picking the appropriate lodging. Transylvania's housing alternatives make sure that your trip is as unforgettable as the area itself, whether you like the elegance of a historic hotel, the warmth of a guesthouse, the camaraderie of a hostel, or the excitement of camping in the wilderness.

DINING AND CUISINE IN TRANSYLVANIA: A Culinary Journey Through Tradition and Flavour

Discovering Transylvania's landscapes and history via exploration is not the only way to experience its rich gastronomic legacy. The delicious taste combination of Transylvanian food is a result of the region's varied background.

We'll take you on a culinary tour of Transylvanian food in this book, including must-eat recipes, regional ingredients, and eating alternatives like restaurants, street food, fine dining, and vegetarian and dietary concerns. We'll also raise a glass to the regional beers, wines, and spirits while showing you around Transylvania's exciting nightlife.

Transylvanian Cuisine

The cuisine of Transylvania is a tapestry made of influences from several historical eras. Its origins are found in the **Saxon**, **German**, **Hungarian**, and **Romanian culinary traditions**, which result in a rich and varied palate. Among the distinctive elements of Transylvanian cuisine are:

a) **Meat-Centric**: Dishes from Transylvania often include meat. Common meats include pork, beef, and fowl, which are often served as robust stews, roasts, and sausages.

b) **Root Vegetables**: The main ingredients in many Transylvanian meals are potatoes and root vegetables including carrots, turnips, and parsnips.

c) **Noodles & Dumplings**: Both galuska (dumplings) and tészta (noodles) are often served as sides to major courses.

Smântână, or sour cream, is a typical ingredient in Transylvanian cooking that gives a variety of foods a richness and tang.

Spices with depth and warmth: Paprika, garlic, and marjoram are widely used to season food.

Sausages: The region of Transylvania is well-known for its sausages, including favorites like mici (grilled sausages) and Sibiu salami.

Must-Try Dishes

Be sure to sample these well-known dishes that perfectly encapsulate the Transylvanian culinary culture while eating there:

I) **Mămăligă** is a hearty cornmeal porridge that is sometimes likened to polenta. It is often served as a side dish with cheese and sour cream on top.

II) **Sarmale**: Perfectly cooked cabbage rolls stuffed with a tasty blend of ground beef, pork, rice, and spices; often served with a dollop of sour cream.

III) **Ciorbă de Burtă:** A substantial soup made with tripe that is sour and seasoned with sour cream and garlic.

IV) **Mici**: Garlic, paprika, and other spices are used to season these tiny, grilled sausages. They're popular at barbecues, and mustard is often used to eat them.

V) **Papanași**: A popular dish consisting of fried doughnuts covered with sour cream and jam, papanași is a delicious delight to sate your hunger.

VI) **Plăcinte**: Savory or sweet pastries, plăcinte may be made with cheese, cabbage, apples, or pumpkin as fillings.

Local flavors and ingredients

The accessibility of regional products and distinctive tastes is a key component of Transylvania's culinary identity. The following ingredients and tastes characterize the cuisine of the area:

Forest Mushrooms: The dense woods of Transylvania are home to a profusion of wild mushrooms that are used in sauces, stews, and soups.

Try some of the regional cheeses, like **caşcaval** and **brânză de burduf**, which are often served with mămăligă or on cheese platters.

Paprika: This spice gives many meals a unique taste, particularly when used in its sweet and smoked versions.

A key component, garlic gives Transylvanian food a strong, fragrant character.

pig: One of the main meat sources in the area, pig is utilized in a variety of dishes, including schnitzels, roasts, and sausages.

Caraway seeds are a typical spice used in Transylvanian cookery to season bread and meats.

Dining Options

Restaurants and Cafes

Cities and villages in Transylvania have a range of eating alternatives, from quaint cafés to eateries providing regional and global cuisine. Here is what to anticipate:

Traditional Restaurants: These places specialize in Romanian and Transylvanian cuisine and provide a flavor of the regional customs.

Cafes: Cafes are great places to relax with a coffee, croissant, or small meal while taking in the atmosphere of the neighborhood.

International food: You may find restaurants providing international fare, including Italian, Chinese, and Mediterranean food, in bigger towns like Cluj-Napoca and Brasov.

Street Food & Markets: Look for neighborhood street food vendors and markets that provide grilled meats, pastries, and munchies for a fast and affordable supper.

Fine Dining Experiences

The fine dining establishments in Transylvania take conventional food to a gourmet level. These eateries provide beautiful food with a contemporary touch and often have a wide range of wines. Major towns like **Cluj-Napoca** and **Brasov** provide fine dining options, giving visitors the chance to enjoy Transylvanian food in a classy atmosphere.

Vegetarian and Dietary Considerations

Travelers who are vegetarian or vegan will discover that Transylvania accommodates their food requirements. Vegetarian alternatives are often available in restaurants, including salads, cheese dishes, and vegetable stews. However, it's wise to specify your dietary needs in detail when placing an order since traditional recipes often include meat or other animal products. You may also discover eateries that specialize in vegetarian and vegan cuisine in bigger cities.

Drink and Nightlife

Locally Made Wines and Spirits

The wine business in Transylvania is booming, with vineyards producing top-notch beverages. The Fetească Neagră and Grasă de Cotnari kinds of local wine, which go well with Transylvanian food, should be tried. Don't pass up the chance to sample classic libations like țuică, a plum brandy, or pălincă, a fruit brandy.

Nightclubs and bars

The nightlife in Transylvania is diverse, with everything from hopping nightclubs to inviting cafés and pubs. The nightlife in big cities like **Cluj-Napoca** and **Brașov** is well-known. Dance to the hottest sounds, enjoy live music or relax with a beverage in a chic lounge. Transylvania's nightlife has something for every taste, so you can relax and mingle with locals after a day of exploring.

The eating and culinary scene in Transylvania is a pleasant investigation of custom and taste, to sum up. Your taste buds will go on a gastronomic exploration, enjoying must-try foods like mămăligă and sarmale as well as learning about regional ingredients and spices.

There is something for every palette in Transylvania's cuisine, whether you choose to eat in a fine dining establishment, enjoy street food, or both. Raise a glass to the region's distinctive wines and spirits, and once the sun goes down, experience the exciting nightlife to make your trip to Transylvania memorable.

PRACTICAL INFORMATION FOR TRAVELING IN TRANSYLVANIA: Navigating Your Journey with Ease

To guarantee a straightforward and comfortable travel, undertaking an adventure in Transylvania involves more than simply enthusiasm. We'll cover topics like money and currency, language and communication, safety and health, local etiquette and customs, internet and connectivity, and accessibility for people with disabilities in this guide to help you navigate Transylvania successfully.

Currency and Money

The official currency of Transylvania is the Romanian Leu (RON) since it is a part of Romania. When vacationing in Transylvania, bear in mind the following important financial and monetary considerations:

a) **Currency Exchange:** In all of Transylvania, banks, exchange offices, and ATMs provide the ability to convert international currencies like Euros or US Dollars.

b) **ATMs**: It is simple to withdraw money in the local currency thanks to the abundance of ATMs in cities and towns. Before you go, ask your bank whether there are any costs for using an overseas ATM.

c) **Credit Cards**: In bigger towns and cities, many hotels, restaurants, and businesses accept major credit cards like Visa and MasterCard. However, for smaller transactions and in more remote regions, it is good to have some cash on hand.

d) **Tipping**: Tipping is expected in Transylvania, with restaurants often expecting between 10% and 15% of the total bill. For outstanding service, you may also provide tips to drivers, hotel employees, and tour guides.

Language and Communication

Romanian is the official language of Transylvania. Although younger people, in particular, use English more and more in metropolitan regions and popular tourist locations, it still helps to be able to communicate in some basic Romanian. Here are some keywords and phrases:

Thank you: Multumesc (Mool-tzoo-mesk)
Yes: Da
No: (Nooh)
Please: (Vah rohg)
Excuse me: Scuzati-ma Skoo-zahtz-ee mah

For easier conversation, having a phrasebook or translation software might be helpful.

Health and Safety

Travelers may feel secure visiting Transylvania. But it's crucial to be educated and use common sense caution:

Emergency Services: Dial 112 for help in case of an emergency.

Healthcare: Major cities often have high-quality medical services. Having travel insurance that includes medical emergencies is advised. Make sure you have any prescriptions and required medicines with you.

Transylvania is a secure site for travelers, but **use care in busy areas** to avoid petty theft. Be mindful of your surroundings and safeguard your possessions.

Natural hazards: If you want to engage in outdoor activities like trekking, be ready for rapidly changing weather, particularly in mountainous areas.

Local Customs and Etiquette

When visiting Transylvania, it is crucial to observe the regional traditions and manners:

A courteous welcome is expected while entering places of commerce and residences. In addition to using titles and last names when greeting somebody at first, a handshake is customary.

When visiting churches and monasteries, dress modestly. Business-casual dress is suited to more formal environments, such as premium restaurants.

Table manners dictate that you should finish everything on your plate while eating and keep your hands at the table rather than on your lap. Avoid leaning your elbows against the table.

When photographing people, always get their consent, particularly in rural locations where people can be more wary.

Religious Sites: Take off your cap and cover your shoulders and knees while entering churches and monasteries. Inside, respect and silence are required.

Internet and Connectivity

Transylvania has typically decent internet connection, particularly in cities. Here are some pointers for keeping in touch:

Wi-Fi: Many hotels, cafés, and restaurants provide their patrons access to free Wi-Fi. Larger towns and cities also have public Wi-Fi hotspots available.

SIM Cards: If you want to use mobile internet often, you may want to get a local SIM card with data. Prepaid SIM cards are available from well-known companies including Orange, Vodafone, and Telekom.

Roaming: To avoid expensive data and call rates, ask your cell operator about your alternatives for foreign roaming.

Accessibility for Travellers with Disability

Transylvania is making efforts to provide accessibility for visitors with impairments, however, it's important to make preparations:

Accommodations: Some inns and motels provide rooms that are accessible. To find out about certain accessibility features, get in touch with them beforehand.

Transportation: Facilities for passengers with disabilities, like ramps and accessible bathrooms, are available at major airports and railway stations. Transport service providers should be informed in advance.

Tourist attractions: There is restricted accessibility at several historical sites and tourist attractions. Do your homework in advance to find out which places provide amenities for those in wheelchairs and other mobility issues.

Language Barrier: Using Romanian words or the help of a native guide or companion may be necessary to communicate particular requirements.

Finally, Transylvania provides a mesmerizing fusion of natural beauty, culture, and history. You may guarantee a pleasurable and trouble-free tour through this alluring area by being knowledgeable about money and currency, language, safety and health, local etiquette, internet and connection, and accessibility. You'll learn that having practical knowledge makes your trip more magical as you explore Transylvania's scenery and immerse yourself in its customs.

TRAVEL RESOURCES TO MAKE YOUR TRANSYLVANIAN ADVENTURE BETTER

Traveling to Transylvania is a thrilling adventure, and having the correct travel tools at your disposal may improve your trip. We'll introduce you to helpful applications and websites in this guide, assist you in making a thorough packing list, and cover the fundamentals of a few languages to enable seamless communication while you're traveling.

Useful websites and apps

Google Maps is an excellent resource for finding your way around Transylvania. You may get details on nearby establishments, modes of public transit, and hiking trails by downloading offline maps for locations with poor connectivity.

Both Booking.com and Airbnb provide a variety of lodging choices in Transylvania, ranging from hotels and guesthouses to unusual lodgings like treehouses and castles.

Use TripAdvisor to browse reviews and suggestions for Transylvania's restaurants, sights to see, and things to do. It's a helpful tool for making travel arrangements.

Use the XE Currency Converter app to stay current on currency exchange rates. It comes in handy when converting pricing from the Romanian Leu to your local currency.

RATUC Cluj: If you're traveling to Cluj-Napoca, this app offers up-to-date information about the city's buses and trams.

Weather applications: To help you plan your activities, check the weather prediction for

Transylvania using applications like Weather.com or AccuWeather.

Although English is the primary language in Transylvania, using a translation program like **Google Translate** may be useful for more sophisticated conversations or for reading menus and signage.

Apps for ride-hailing: In several Transylvanian cities, apps like Uber and Bolt (formerly Taxify) are accessible and useful for traveling.

Download trail maps for certain Transylvanian districts or parks if you want to go hiking. Excellent options include apps like Maps.me or AllTrails.

Package List

Make a thorough packing list to make sure you're ready for your Transylvanian excursion. Here is a list of crucial factors to think about:

Travel Documents

A passport and a visa, if necessary
Traveling insurance papers
Tickets for flights or trains and a schedule
copies of significant documents

Clothing:

Proper attire for the weather (layers for changing temperatures)
Commodious hiking boots or walking shoes
Poncho or raincoat
Shades and a hat (If attending thermal spas)
Swimwear

Travel equipment

Daypack or a backpack
Chargers and adapters for travel
Cellular power supply
Portable toiletries
Used water bottle
Travel poncho

Safety and Health

copies of prescriptions and prescription drugs
First-aid supply
insect repellent Lip balm with SPF, sunscreen, and other over-the-counter essentials

Miscellaneous

A travel manual or maps
The use of a travel cushion and eye mask
accessories and a camera

(For storing and arranging stuff) Ziplock bags Laundry detergent for travelers (for washing clothing while traveling)

Language basic

Even if English is widely spoken in tourist locations, learning a few fundamental Romanian words may improve your trip and demonstrate respect for the local way of life.

In conclusion, Transylvania provides a variety of adventures, like trekking through beautiful landscapes and discovering old castles. You'll be ready to make the most of your trip through this captivating area if you have access to the necessary travel tools, such as useful apps and websites, a well-planned packing list, and a working knowledge of the local tongue.

APPENDIX: Essential Reference for Your Transylvanian Journey

We've gathered basic information about Transylvania, a glossary of words to assist you in exploring the area, and crucial emergency numbers to keep you safe while traveling in this appendix.

Quick Facts about Transylvania

Central Romania contains the historical area of Transylvania. The Carpathian Mountains encircle it on the east and south.

Capital: Cluj-Napoca, one of Transylvania's main cities, is a significant center for both culture and commerce.

Languages: Romanian is the official language. Even though English is widely spoken in tourist regions, learning a few fundamental Romanian words is helpful.

The Romanian Leu **(RON)** is the official currency.

Transylvania has a continental climate, which has four distinct seasons. Warm summers alternate with cold, snowy winters, particularly in mountainous regions.

Eastern European Summer Time (EEST), which is UTC+3, and Eastern European Time (EET), which is UTC+2, are the time zones in use in Transylvania.

Transylvania is well-known for its ancient cities, castles (particularly Bran Castle, which is sometimes linked to Dracula), and picturesque scenery, notably the Carpathian Mountains.

Food: Hearty foods like mămăligă (cornmeal porridge), sarmale (cabbage rolls), and regional cheeses are typical of Transylvanian cuisine. Try the traditional țuică (plum brandy) without fail.

Glossary of Common Terms
Buna ziua: Hello
Multumesc: thank you.
Da: Yes
Nu: No
Va rog: Please
Scuzati-ma: Excuse me
La revedere: Goodbye
Sarmale: Rice and meat-filled cabbage rolls
Castel: Castle
Biserica: Church
Mountain: Munte
City: Oras
Sat: Village
Lake: Lac
Autogara: Bus station
Train station: Gara
Market or square: Piața

Street: Strada

Bani: Money

Emergency Contacts

Although Transylvania is typically secure for tourists, it's important to know who to contact in case of an emergency:

For police, **fire**, or **medical** situations, dial 112 for emergency services. This number is functional throughout Europe.

Medical Emergencies: In the event of a medical emergency, you may also dial 112 or go to the closest hospital or healthcare institution for help.

Find your country's embassy or consulate in Romania if you're a foreign citizen in need of help with passport-related matters or other consular services.

Lost or Stolen Passport: Report a lost or stolen passport right away to the embassy or consulate of your nation. They may help with replacement and provide instructions on essential steps.

Local Police: For help or to report minor offenses in non-emergency circumstances, get in touch with your neighborhood police department.

Keep your travel insurance policy and contact details close to hand in case you need to file a claim or seek help for travel delays, medical emergencies, or misplaced possessions.

You'll be better prepared to traverse Transylvania and have a safe and enjoyable trip through this fascinating area if you are acquainted with some basic information, common words, and emergency contacts.

CONCLUSION: Farewell to Transylvania, Until We Meet Again

We hope that the **Transylvania Travel Guide 2023** voyage has been an inspiration and a source of useful information, helping you to experience the enchantment of this captivating Romanian province. There is no question that the scenery, castles, and culture of Transylvania have permanently etched themselves into your heart.

Transylvania has given you a taste of its distinct appeal whether you've meandered through ancient alleys, enjoyed regional food, or experienced the spectacular natural splendor of the Carpathian Mountains.

But keep in mind that Transylvania will always be an amazing destination, ready to welcome you back for further exploration. Until that time, may your recollections of this fabled place be warm, exciting, and a yearning for the day when you might once again wander its cobblestone streets and discover its hidden treasures. Till we meet again in the embrace of Transylvania, farewell, sweet wanderer.

WHEN VISITING TRANSYLVANIA, AVOID THESE 15 THINGS AT ALL COSTS.

It's an exciting experience to go to Transylvania, but it's important to respect the indigenous way of life. 15 things not to do when seeing this fascinating Romanian area are listed below:

Don't Make Dracula Jokes: Dracula's connection to Transylvania is a delicate subject. Do not trivialize it or stereotype the area.

Respect religious sites by dressing modestly and acting respectfully when you enter churches and monasteries.

Avoid littering; Transylvania's natural beauty has to be preserved. Follow the Leave No Trace principles and dispose of rubbish correctly.

Avoid Being Aggressive When Bargaining: Bargaining is usual in marketplaces, but always be kind and considerate when discussing costs.

Flash photography may harm artwork and antiques, so abide by museum guidelines and refrain from using it there.

Avoid Making Public Displays of Love: In Transylvania, it is preferable to avoid making overt displays of love.

Don't Skip Local Cuisine: Try local specialties that aren't as well known to you, such as sarmale and mămăligă.

Respect Private Property: When photographing individuals in rural regions or invading private premises, get permission first.

Don't Disrupt Wildlife: If you like seeing wildlife, stay your distance and try to avoid disturbing the animals.

Avoid Political Discussions: It is advisable to concentrate on cultural exchanges and vacation experiences rather than talking about delicate political issues.

Don't Assume Everyone Speaks English: While English is often spoken in tourist regions, it might be useful to learn a few simple Romanian words.

Respect for Gypsy Communities: It is rude and disrespectful to stereotype or stigmatize the Roma (Gypsy) communities.

Avoid Wasting Resources: Be aware of your water and energy use, particularly in rural locations where resources may be scarce.

Don't Ignore Local Customs: Get acquainted with regional customs, such as taking off your shoes while entering someone's house.

Don't Rush: The attraction of Transylvania rests in its leisurely pace. Take your time, relish each second, and let the beauty of it wash over you.

You may ensure a courteous and educational experience while discovering Transylvania's riches by being aware of these factors.

(HAPPY TRAVELS)

Printed in Great Britain
by Amazon